Hedge Fund
Trading Strategies
Detailed Explanation Of
ETF Dividend Pirating

AN INVESTING NEWSLETTER

HEDGE STRATEGIES

™

...offering impersonal, general and indirect opinion

An
Aggressive Strategy
And Bonus Report

ISBN 1451514808
EAN 978-1-451-51480-3

1. Hedge-Fund 2. Hedgefund 3. Derivatives 4. ETF
5. Exchange-Traded-Fund 6. Options 7. Investing
8. Strategies 9. Trading 10. Dividend

Printed in the United States of America

Hedge Strategies
…an investing newsletter of general, impersonal and indirect opinion

STRATEGY DESCRIPTION AND EXPLANATION
For
ETF Dividend Pirating, an Aggressive Strategy

> When a company declares that a stock dividend will be paid, it establishes a date on which the owners of its stock will be recorded to determine to whom to pay the dividend. Stock sales require three business days after a purchase to settle and record the new owner of the stock. The day following the last date that one can purchase a stock and be recorded as its owner of record is the Ex-Date. 'Ex' refers to 'without', meaning that the stock now trades without the rights to its dividend. On Ex-Date the stock price will open lower by the amount of the declared dividend. This is a function of the exchange, not of the forces of the market (buyers and sellers), because the dividend and its value no longer accompany the stock.
>
> Pirating an ETF dividend should not be confused with 'selling a stock dividend'. Selling a stock dividend was an unethical practice used by stockbrokers to increase commissions. They would recommend that their client purchase a stock because it was going to pay a dividend. This allowed the stockbroker to earn two commissions for their brokerage—one on the purchase of the stock and one on the sale of the stock. This practice was banned by the Securities and Exchange Commission (SEC) in 1934, because the stock price is adjusted lower the following morning (its Ex-Date). The stock is sellable by an amount minus its dividend, netting a zero gain on the transaction for the client, but churning commission fees for the broker and his brokerage.

This report outlines an aggressive strategy that seeks to take the dividend from an investment with the least amount of price exposure, as measured by time spent in or owning the investment.

What Is An ETF?
ETF stands for exchange traded fund. These securities trade like stocks on an exchange. The ETF is composed of a basket of individual stocks. Index ETFs seek to mimic an index by holding the group of stocks that compose the index in an appropriate proportion to cause the value of an index ETF to move in tandem with the actual index to an accuracy (correlation) of 98% or greater. Indices are the Dow Jones Industrial Average, Standard & Poor's 500, Nasdaq 100, Wilshire 1000 and Russell 2000, to name a few.

Index ETF values are a fraction of their mimicked index value. For example, the ticker symbol SPY, the index ETF mimicking the Standard and Poor's 500 Index, is $1/10^{th}$ the value of the index. If the Standard and Poor's 500 Index is 1000, the SPY will be trading at approximately 100. By definition, indices are diversified, therefore Index ETFs are diversified. Index ETFs like the SPY, DIA and QQQQ representing the Standard and Poor's 500 Index, the Dow Jones Industrial Average and the NASDAQ 100 experience high levels of daily trading volume.

What cannot be done with stocks can be done with ETFs. ETFs are not stocks. Though ETFs also pay a dividend, from the dividends of the stocks in the ETF's portfolio, the ETF does not open lower by the amount of the declared dividend. The ETF derives its value from only the market prices of the stocks in its portfolio (plus a small valuation adjustment). Moreover, not all of the stocks in the ETF's portfolio declare dividends on the same days in the same weeks of the same months.

The ETF accumulates the dividends of its portfolio stocks and pays them to holders of ETF shares monthly, quarterly, semi-annually or annually.

The ETF value change related to the declaration of the dividends for the stocks in its portfolio has already occurred, as reflected in the daily prices of its portfolio stocks, that were averaged to derive the trading value of the ETF. There is no required decrease in the market price of the ETF on its Ex-Date after it records to whom it will pay the dividends of its portfolio stocks. This is the opportunity!

What Is Correlation?

Correlation is a measure of how similarly or differently the prices of two securities move in the market. Negative correlations mean that the security prices move in opposite directions. For example, if a gold commodity ETF has a negative correlation to an index ETF of -0.5, the gold commodity ETF generally moves half of the percentage price movement of the index ETF in the opposite direction. In other words, when the index ETF price moves up 1%, the gold commodity ETF price moves down ½%. Positive correlations mean that the security prices move similarly to each other. The prices of two securities move exactly the same if their correlation is +1.

What Is The Breakeven Point?

The breakeven point is a calculation providing the price at which the investment begins to lose money.

How Is The Breakeven Point Determined?

The breakeven point is determined by the calculation:

> ETF Acquiring Price – Pirated Dividend + Cost of Trades = Breakeven Point

What Is The Way To Profit?

At market opening on Ex-Date, the day that the ETF no longer trades with its dividend, the ETF must be sold for no less than the amount for which it was purchased the previous day, minus the pirated dividend, plus the trading costs, i.e., above its breakeven point.

What Are The Risks?

The psychological impact of a national news story might overnight cause the ETF to open below the prior day's acquiring price. This phenomenon is called *gapping down*. Other pirates will also be attempting to unload their ETFs as soon as possible, which can cause supply forces to gap an ETF's market price.

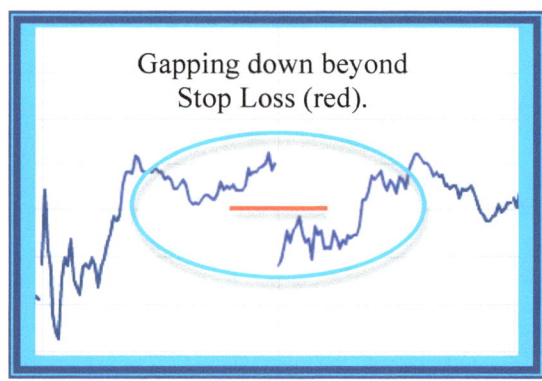

Gapping down beyond Stop Loss (red).

These scenarios can cause the ETF's market price to move down so far so fast that an applied stop loss order sells the investment to the market at opening bell lower than desired, causing a loss greater than planned. If either scenario were to occur, there would be immediate value loss unless two events occur: (1) the stop loss is deactivated or converted to a trailing stop, and then (2) the market price of the ETF returns to at least the breakeven point, where it can be sold back to the market at a zero sum gain/loss.

The stop loss deactivation decision is not left to chance, but is predetermined based on the overnight movement of market futures, pre-market price averages and other indicators.

What Is The Reward?

Best-case results can yield dividend returns of over 45% annually, plus any incidental appreciation of the ETF market price experienced from exposure to market activity. If the ETF experiences a *gap up* in price, that is considered incidental price appreciation.

The Strategy Rules, in Order of Importance
(1) Trade only ETFs that are correlative with market conditions that rise in value.
(2) Trade only ETFs with high levels of trading volume, liquidity and diversification.
(3) Never remain in a pirated ETF for its dividend longer than one trading day.
(4) Never deviate from the Guidemaps.

Outline Of An Aggressive Strategy: ETF Dividend Pirating
There are two components to this ETF dividend pirating strategy: the entry trade and the exit trade. The cost of these trades is not factored into return percentages, but can be calculated as a fixed amount of $3.00 per action regardless of share quantity. Buying the ETF is an action, and selling the ETF is an action. A transaction of 1 or 100 or 1000 shares will cost $3.00 per action.

Entry Strategy
Step 1: Purchase ETF for its dividend income.
Step 2: Establish either the stop loss or the trailing stop loss.

Exit Strategy
Step 3: Sell the ETF back to the market on Ex-Date with a sell limit order at the ETF acquiring price.
Step 4: Make appropriate early morning adjustments, possibly requiring the ETF investment to spend additional time in the market before its sale is executed.

Technical Indicator Guidemap
Technical Indicators determine if the market conditions are bearish (going down) or bullish (going up). It is better that the stop loss be shallower during a bearish condition, and deeper during a bullish condition. Prices move down with greater speed than they move up. When the ETF breaches the price point of the stop loss in a market with bearish sentiment, continuing declines are likely, making it better to exit sooner rather than later. A deeper stop loss is recommended during markets with bullish sentiment because price drops often reverse and move positive (higher than the point of entry) during the course of the trading day.

Selection Of The ETF Guidemap
The direction by which the ETF investment is likely to move is predicted using the variables of (i) technical indicators, (ii) market sentiment, (iii) market volatility, (iv) the overnight and pre-market movement of market futures, and (v) the release of news.

The pirated ETF is held for a very short period of time (most likely overnight, but no longer than one day). The type of ETF selected is determined by the current market sentiment and its correlation to the market. The market price of any stock that provides a dividend will open the following day lower by the amount of its stock dividend. Historically, this is not the case for ETF investments.

Sentiment Correlation Of Pirated ETF Guidemap

Choosing a high yielding ETF positively correlated to the market or a moderate yielding ETF negatively correlated to the market is determined by either the bearish or bullish sentiment of the market at that time. Though the ETF is held for a very short period of time, unfavorable daily price swings of the selected ETF can erode the investment principal, making this effort unprofitable if unhedged.

This is particularly true when selecting the higher yielding ETFs that can suffer from potential gap downs and investment price erosion at a high rate when the market is bearish. Therefore, when the market sentiment is bullish, the higher yielding ETFs will be selected. When the market sentiment is bearish, the moderate yielding, negatively correlated ETFs will be selected to counteract possible downward market movements.

Stop Loss Percentage Guidemap

If at market opening the market price of the ETF gaps down below the breakeven point, losses of ETF investment principal will occur. Minimize possible continuing losses by applying a stop loss order to the ETF investment. The stop loss will close the ETF investment by selling it to the market at its opening or current price. The stop loss is shallower in a bearish market than in a bullish market as determined by the Technical Indicator Guidemap, because a downturn in a bullish market at opening will likely reverse itself within the first hour of the trading session, making a below breakeven sale of the ETF unnecessary. Establish the stop loss at the ETF breakeven point for the anticipated change in direction during a bullish market, and one-half of the breakeven amount during an uncommitted or bearish market.

At market opening the stop loss will be deactivated and changed to a trailing stop at the ETF acquiring price when market volatility is low relative to its recent 1-week average, and market sentiment is bullish. The trailing stop allows for the upside appreciation of the ETF investment. It will trigger the sale of the ETF investment if it begins to backtrack (give back) its session gains.

For example:

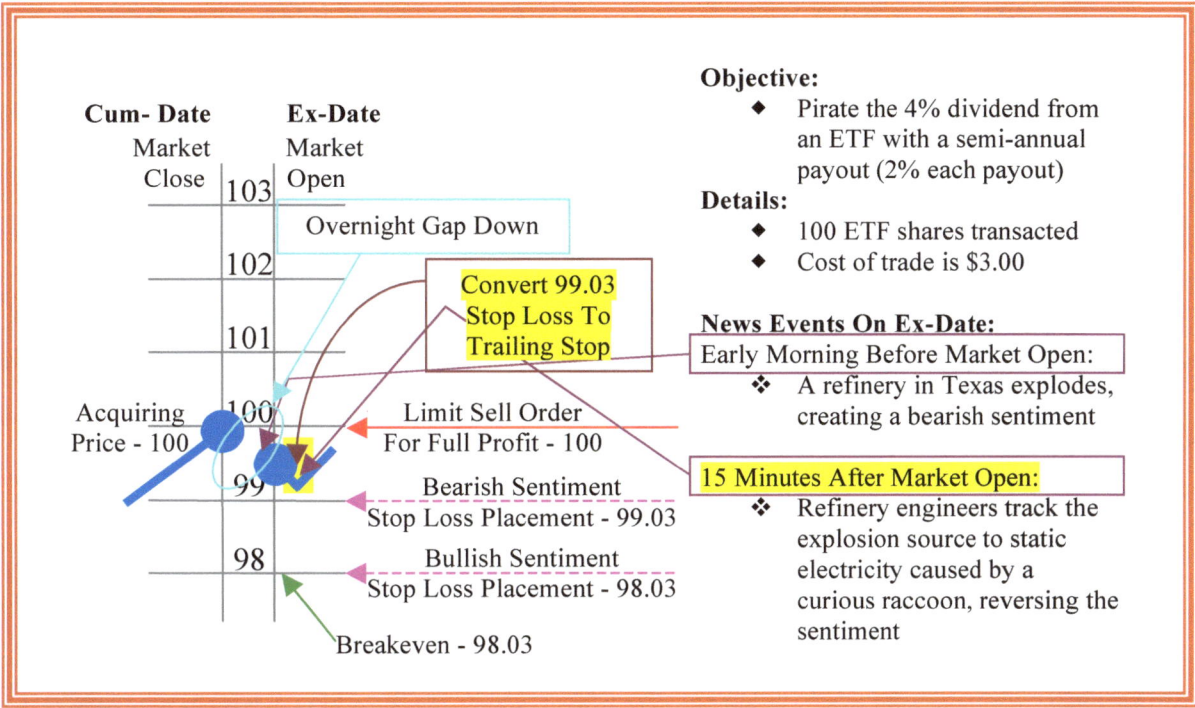

Objective:
- Pirate the 4% dividend from an ETF with a semi-annual payout (2% each payout)

Details:
- 100 ETF shares transacted
- Cost of trade is $3.00

News Events On Ex-Date:

Early Morning Before Market Open:
- ❖ A refinery in Texas explodes, creating a bearish sentiment

15 Minutes After Market Open:
- ❖ Refinery engineers track the explosion source to static electricity caused by a curious raccoon, reversing the sentiment

Diagram labels:

Cum-Date — Market Close | Ex-Date — Market Open

103, 102, 101, 100, 99, 98

Overnight Gap Down

Convert 99.03 Stop Loss To Trailing Stop

Acquiring Price - 100

Limit Sell Order For Full Profit - 100

Bearish Sentiment Stop Loss Placement - 99.03

Bullish Sentiment Stop Loss Placement - 98.03

Breakeven - 98.03

Stay With The ETF A Little Longer Guidemap

The ETF can be held for longer than the opening bell on its Ex-Date trading day if market futures indicate bullish sentiment and the ETF market price appreciation is protected with a trailing stop set at the ETF acquiring price.

This Strategy Put To The Test

ETFs are selected for purchase based on their potential for dividend income and zero loss of investment. Twelve dividend delivering ETFs (A through L) are selected. Some are traded just once per year. Others are traded regularly depending on the frequency of their dividend distribution.

On the Ex-Date the ETF will be sold back to the market. There is no reason to hold the ETF longer than the market opening, other than for upside appreciation potential resulting from the conversion of the stop loss to a trailing stop at the ETF acquiring price when Guidemaps deem it appropriate.

The following chart shows the practical results of this strategy over one year. ETF A in the month of January has its Ex-Date on January 16, with a paid dividend return of 0.17%. December by contrast is quite active in that ETF B is sold back to the market on the 1st. Then, ETF K is purchased on the day prior to its Ex-Date of the 18th, and is sold back to the market the following trading day. ETF F is purchased on the day prior to its Ex-Date of the 22nd. On the 22nd ETF F is sold back to the market and that same day replaced by ETF J, which is purchased at closing bell. ETF J is sold back to the market on the 23rd and replaced by ETF D.

Each time these ETFs are purchased, they are sold the following trading day at the opening bell quoted price, after being held overnight just long enough to acquire the rights to their dividends.

	JAN 09		FEB 09		MAR 09		APR 09		MAY 09		JNE 09	
	Ex-Date	Return	Ex-Date	Return	Ex-Date	Return	Ex-Date	Return	Ex-Date	Return	Ex-Date	Return
ETF A	16	0.17%	20	0.49%			17	0.16%	15	0.29%		
ETF B			2	1.12%					1	1.24%	1	1.17%
ETF C					20	0.71%						
ETF D					25	1.37%					23	1.70%
ETF E					24	1.79%						
ETF F											22	2.59%
ETF G											24	1.49%
ETF H												
ETF I												
ETF J												
ETF K											19	2.38%
ETF L					2	0.28%	1	0.27%				
Monthly Returns	0.17%		1.61%		4.15%		0.44%		1.54%		9.33%	

	JLY 09		AUG 09		SEP 08		OCT 08		NOV 08		DEC 08	
	Ex-Date	Return	Ex-Date	Return	Ex-Date	Return	Ex-Date	Return	Ex-Date	Return	Ex-Date	Return
ETF A	17	0.14%	21	0.35%			17	0.17%	21	0.45%		
ETF B			3	1.10%	2	0.81%			3	1.16%	1	1.32%
ETF C					19	0.58%						
ETF D											24	4.92%
ETF E												
ETF F											22	3.04%
ETF G					24	1.26%						
ETF H	2	0.71%										
ETF I					21	1.53%						
ETF J											23	7.59%
ETF K											18	3.63%
ETF L	1	0.32%									29	0.33%
Monthly Returns	1.18%		1.45%		4.18%		0.17%		1.61%		20.84%	

Dividend Return	46.67%

If the prior day's ETF closing price is the price at which the ETF is sold back to the market on its Ex-Date, the hypothesis of this practical example states that the target and actual return from the pirated dividends is 46.67%. This is not always the case, as seen in the following chart results. Why? Gapping down and the presence of other dividend pirates forces lower price openings, skewing the ETF's net asset value.

Some pirates have the advantage of getting their ETF share sell orders in before others. The gapping down events prove it. They are able to queue their sale prices with the exchange's market makers to unload Ex-Date ETFs in pre-market trading before the market opens and to be first-in-line to be matched with higher price buyers at opening bell. There is a solution to being left in line waiting to sell dividend pirated ETF shares that will be explained at the end of the results analysis in *The Solution For Pesky Pirates* section.

When viewing the following chart of results, note the following: (1) the value of the ETFs' Ex-Date gapping (purple arrow) is listed beside Market Sentiment; (2) the variance of the broad market as measured by the S&P 500 Index (symbol: ^gspc, orange arrow) showing its gapping activity on the ETFs' Ex-Date; (3) the net result of dividends and gappings are accumulated as Monthly Returns (green circle).

	JAN 09			^gspc	FEB 09			^gspc	MAR 09			^gspc
	Market Sentiment	Gapping Gain/Loss	Div & Gap Net	Market Gain/Loss	Market Sentiment	Gapping Gain/Loss	Div & Gap Net	Market Gain/Loss	Market Sentiment	Gapping Gain/Loss	Div & Gap Net	Market Gain/Loss
ETF A	Bearish	1.25%	1.42%	0.08%	Bearish	-2.33%	-1.85%	-0.39%				
ETF B					Bullish	-1.89%	-0.77%	-0.34%				
ETF C									Bullish	-0.23%	0.48%	0.06%
ETF D									Bullish	3.17%	4.54%	0.85%
ETF E									Bullish	-4.40%	-2.61%	-0.28%
ETF L									Bearish	0.33%	0.61%	-0.76%
Monthly Returns		1.42%		0.08%		-2.61%		-0.73%		3.02%		-0.13%

	APR 09			^gspc	MAY 09			^gspc	JNE 09			^gspc
	Market Sentiment	Gapping Gain/Loss	Div & Gap Net	Market Gain/Loss	Market Sentiment	Gapping Gain/Loss	Div & Gap Net	Market Gain/Loss	Market Sentiment	Gapping Gain/Loss	Div & Gap Net	Market Gain/Loss
ETF A	Bullish	0.22%	0.39%	-0.01%	Bearish	-0.29%	0.01%	-0.03%				
ETF B					Bullish	-0.42%	0.82%	-0.01%	Bullish	-0.49%	0.68%	0.45%
ETF D									Bearish	-0.55%	1.15%	0.37%
ETF F									Bearish	-3.37%	-0.78%	-0.34%
ETF G									Bearish	-0.03%	1.46%	0.14%
ETF K									Bearish	-1.02%	1.36%	0.17%
ETF L	Bearish	0.26%	0.53%	-0.54%								
Monthly Returns		0.92%		-0.55%		0.83%		-0.04%		3.87%		0.79%

	JLY 09			^gspc	AUG 09			^gspc	SEP 08			^gspc
	Market Sentiment	Gapping Gain/Loss	Div & Gap Net	Market Gain/Loss	Market Sentiment	Gapping Gain/Loss	Div & Gap Net	Market Gain/Loss	Market Sentiment	Gapping Gain/Loss	Div & Gap Net	Market Gain/Loss
ETF A	Bullish	-0.01%	0.13%	-0.02%	Bearish	0.20%	0.55%	0.17%				
ETF B					Bullish	-0.73%	0.36%	0.28%	Bullish	-0.21%	0.60%	0.33%
ETF C									Bearish	5.23%	5.81%	0.55%
ETF G									Bearish	0.53%	1.80%	0.05%
ETF H	Bullish	-2.21%	-1.49%	-0.16%								
ETF I									Bearish	-0.67%	0.86%	0.02%
ETF L	Bearish	-1.23%	-0.91%	0.17%								
Monthly Returns	-2.27%			-0.01%	0.92%			0.45%	9.06%			0.95%

	OCT 08			^gspc	NOV 08			^gspc	DEC 08			^gspc
	Market Sentiment	Gapping Gain/Loss	Div & Gap Net	Market Gain/Loss	Market Sentiment	Gapping Gain/Loss	Div & Gap Net	Market Gain/Loss	Market Sentiment	Gapping Gain/Loss	Div & Gap Net	Market Gain/Loss
ETF A	Bullish	-2.59%	-2.42%	-0.44%	Bearish	1.39%	1.84%	0.45%				
ETF B					Bullish	1.04%	2.20%	-0.01%	Bullish	-0.82%	0.50%	-0.86%
ETF D									Bullish	-3.82%	1.10%	0.08%
ETF F									Bullish	-2.55%	0.49%	-0.08%
ETF J									Bullish	-10.29%	-2.70%	0.31%
ETF K									Bullish	-4.93%	-1.30%	0.17%
ETF L									Bearish	0.11%	0.44%	-0.05%
Monthly Returns	-2.42%			-0.44%	4.04%			0.44%	-1.46%			-0.43%

Annual Return	15.32%

The closing price on the previous trading day was the price at which the ETF is purchased. The market opening price on Ex-Date was the price at which the ETF is sold back to the market. The results marked by the red boxes indicate that certain ETFs experienced degrees of gapping which made the attempt at piracy unprofitable. An advantage is needed to sell certain ETFs back to the market on their Ex-Date ahead of others attempting to do the same. Standard retail trading platforms do not provide that advantage. A professional trading platform is required (see section *The Faster Ship Advantage* for further explanation).

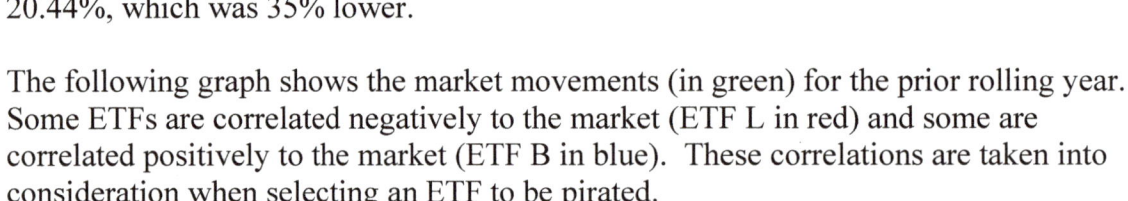

The ETF Dividend Pirating aggressive strategy produced a return of 15.32% (light blue squares, following chart) during the rolling year tested, ending August 28, 2009. By comparison, the broad market return as measure by the S&P 500 Index (symbol: ^gspc in green) produced a result of -20.44%, which was 35% lower.

The following graph shows the market movements (in green) for the prior rolling year. Some ETFs are correlated negatively to the market (ETF L in red) and some are correlated positively to the market (ETF B in blue). These correlations are taken into consideration when selecting an ETF to be pirated.

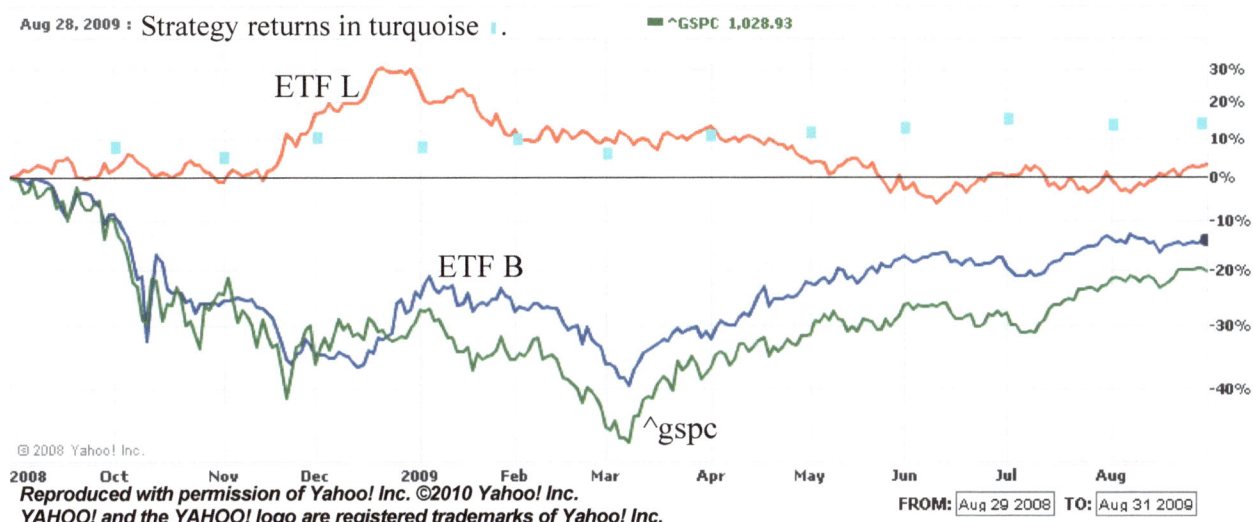

Why It's Done This Way

Remember, profits are made only through a sale, never a purchase. Holding onto a security for more than the least amount of time possible exposes an unhedged investment to both loss of principal and loss of dividend profit. The stop loss and trailing stop can protect the investment through a quick sale back to the market, but if gapping down occurs on Ex-Date, the opportunity to pirate dividends with the least amount of exposure to systematic market risk is missed. If the ETF is purchased at the close of trading the day before Ex-Date and sold at the opening bell on its Ex-Date, the amount of time the ETF investment is exposed to the market is seconds.

The Faster Ship Advantage

The results of this ETF dividend pirating strategy in the chart above are positive, considering that the broad market return for this same period was -20.44%. However, 67% of this strategy's potential profit was lost because the trading market was not equal to all participants as measured by the opening prices of the ETFs tested. Fortunately, this strategy can be facilitated by accessing professional trading platforms that are able to place sell orders ahead of regular market hours sell orders through two advantages: (1) pre-market trading is available to it before the market opens, allowing ETF shares to be matched and sold to buyers before regular market hours traders have the opportunity to sell their ETF shares; (2) trading algorithms place the ETF sell orders aggressively ahead of others for execution at market opening by splitting ETF share quantities and averaging order prices when an acceptable share price selling range is submitted. These advantages make for a faster pirate ship.

The Solution For Pesky Pirates - A Hedging Option

This strategy can improve success by countering the overnight gapping experienced by the ETFs' market prices. How? With a derivative hedge.

What Is A Hedge?

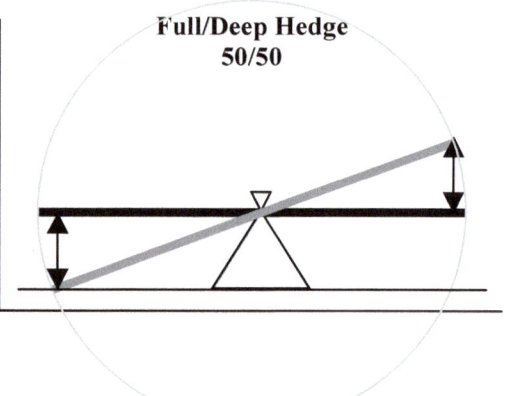

A hedge is an act, tool or means of preventing loss in one security with another partially or fully counter-balancing security. A hedge reduces the possibility of a loss of principal (value) due to adverse movements of the investment or position. A hedge may be realized through purchases of counter-balancing securities as well as through sales of counter-balancing securities.

For example: A hedge is considered to be *full, perfect, deep* or *counter-balancing* when there is no loss in value from price movements. A *shallow hedge* experiences loss in value from price movements.

When the market fills with pirates creating stiff competition, the smarter pirate improvises to hedge his market exposure through use of derivatives and arbitrage, in addition to utilizing the advantages of fast and smarter professional trading platforms.

What Are Derivatives?

Derivatives are contracts or obligations that are bought or sold in trading markets. They derive their value from the movement of other securities, such as stocks, exchange traded funds (ETFs), bonds, commodities or currencies. Options are derivatives.

Take a page from the Hedge Strategies report, *Hedged Income ETF, a Conservative Strategy* (also available on the Hedge Strategies website) which uses sold call options to hedge downside risk while providing leverage to returns. For example, September 2, 2009, was the most recent Ex-Date for dividend paying ETFs after the rolling year example that ended August 28, 2009. All ETFs offering dividends on September 2 experienced gap downs. The broad market as measured by the S&P 500 Index experienced an insignificant gap down of .01%. Observing the positively correlated and negatively correlated ETFs, it is evident that the dividend opportunity of both types of ETFs was traded away by pirates.

The solution is to sell a call option for the underlying ETF with high trading volume, narrow spreads and sufficient time value (speculative value) to equal at least the amount of the anticipated dividend. As applied in the chart below, identified by the red circle, the results for ETF L eliminated the pre-hedge losses of -.44 per share.

The sold call hedge when applied to ETF M not only eliminated the gapping, but also provided additional income, leveraging the return from 0.60% to 1.04%, due to the collapse of implied volatility as reflected in the premium of this particular call option. As a rule never buy a hedge; it involves great expense, provides unnecessary protection for a time period of seconds, and suffers deterioration of value over time (even in as short a period as overnight, as exemplified below in the collapse of implied volatility of the ETF M sold call option which provided excess profit of 0.13 per share for the hedge, calculated as follows:

0.35 (The Sold Call Gapping Amount) − 0.22 (The ETF's Gapping Amount)

The results of this hedging option appear in the following chart.

SEP 09 ETF L Price Per Share					Net Hedged Result
Prior Date Purchase	Ex-Date Open	Gapping Gain/Loss	Pirated Dividend	Net Result	
96.60	95.85	-0.75	0.31	-0.44	
SEP 09 Sold Call Option Price Per ETF L Share					
Prior Date Purchase	Ex-Date Open	Gapping Gain/Loss	--	Net Result	0.01
1.60	1.15	0.45	--	0.45	

SEP 09 ETF M Price Per Share					Net Hedged Result
Prior Date Purchase	Ex-Date Open	Gapping Gain/Loss	Pirated Dividend	Net Result	
34.70	34.48	-0.22	0.22	0.00	
SEP 09 Sold Call Option Price Per ETF M Share					
Prior Date Purchase	Ex-Date Open	Gapping Gain/Loss	--	Net Result	0.35
1.15	0.8	0.35	--	0.35	

Applying anti-gapping derivative hedges to ETFs targeted for pirating can counter the negative results of price gap downs. This opportunity is discussed in more detail in the Hedge Strategies report Event Driven Volatility Capturing Hedged Profit Spreads, available at the Hedge Strategies website, *www.HedgeStrategies.info*.

Looking Forward

Incorporate the use of a hedging call option and this aggressive strategy can be broadened to pirate the dividends of ETFs on trading exchanges globally. There are numerous exchanges in countries around the world that trade options on their ETF listings.

Typically in any month, the investment principal used in this strategy is idle 85% of the time. Look at the chart on page 10, which shows the availability of investment principal for global overnight pirating and other strategies.

Questions regarding this material may be forwarded to help3edp@HedgeStrategies.info.

Additional Hedge Strategies Investing Reports

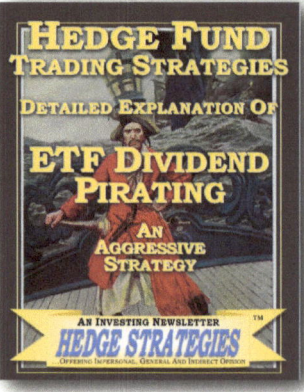

RISK DISCLOSURE STATEMENT

It should not be assumed that concepts, models or strategies discussed, presently or in the future, will always be profitable or will equal the performance of the strategy as explained in this report.

Transactions in options carry a high degree of risk. If the option is "covered" by the seller holding a corresponding position in the underlying security or a future contract or another option, the risk may be reduced. If the option is not covered, the risk of loss can be unlimited.

Most open-outcry and electronic trading facilities are supported by computer-based component systems for the order routing, execution, matching, registration or clearing of trades. As with all facilities and systems, they are vulnerable to temporary disruption or failure. Your ability to recover certain losses may be subject to limits on liability imposed by the system provider, the market, the clearing house and/or member firms. Such limits may vary. You can ask the firm with which you deal for details in this respect.

Trading on an electronic trading system may differ not only from trading in an open-outcry market, but also from trading on other electronic trading systems. If you undertake transactions on an electronic trading system, you will be exposed to risks associated with the system including the failure of hardware and software. The result of any system failure may be that your order is either not executed according to your instructions or is not executed at all.

There is a winner and a loser in every market transaction. More often than not, the winners are the wealthy who can afford the services of the financial industries' best and brightest, and the losers are the average American who can invest only in mutual funds, stocks and sometimes bonds. When the market fell during the 2007 -2009 recession, hedged investments were making money while unhedged investments (those investments available to the average American) were losing money. The wealthy became wealthier and the average American became poorer.

One may have heard that:

- A buy and hold strategy will beat a strategy that employs market timing techniques.
- Mutual funds and variable life insurance are safe vehicles for investment dollars.
- Leverage is risky.

These statements are inaccurate propaganda broadcast by the mutual fund and life insurance industries.

There was a time when the tobacco companies advertised on television. Those advertisements often claimed that smoking benefited one's well-being. Now with universal knowledge of the dangers of tobacco products, those claims would never be trusted. Likewise, it is time that the claims of the financial services industry are questioned.

Today, many believe that mutual funds and life insurance are the best investments for their dollars. The entire financial planning and advisory industries exist because they successfully broadcast these inaccurate claims. Not all life insurance is a bad investment and not all mutual funds poor performers, but the majority do not beat their benchmark index. And none (except those that are not specifically managed as bear market or short funds) makes money when the market falls.

The figures presented by the mutual fund industry claim that only about 35% of mutual funds fail to meet or beat the benchmark return average. This is not a flat lie, but it withholds the entire truth about mutual fund performance.

Mutual funds that have failed and closed, or failed and have been rolled into another mutual fund are not included. Include all failed mutual funds and over 90% fail to meet or beat the benchmark return average. Which 10% are the best? No one knows. The mutual fund industry's claims are derived with error in its data set, which fails to include the dead or failed mutual funds. This type of error is caller *survivor bias*.

Change is difficult and obstacles to leveling the financial playing field are great. The wealthiest and most powerful Americans do not want to share their prosperity with the average American.

It bears repeating, there is always a *winner* and a *loser* in every market transaction. The winners accumulate profits or eliminate losses when others suffer losses. Losers face *barriers to access* the best investment vehicles for their investment dollars. A barrier to access also is believing and acting upon inaccurate information supplied by the mutual fund industry, the life insurance industry and the planning and advisory industry that promotes and sells mutual fund and life insurance products.

Before one can learn techniques for timing the market and trend trading, one must believe the false assertion that market timing efforts are futile, is itself based on the desire of the industries to confuse and discourage change in the average American's investing behavior.

Mutual fund and life insurance industries do not want average Americans to change their investing beliefs and behavior because these industries make enormous amounts of money at the average American's expense. The average American's investing disadvantage is also fueling the affluent's growing wealth.

Those with a rudimentary knowledge of how exchanges work (like the New York Stock Exchange or the Chicago Board Option Exchange) argue that it is the market maker that gets stuck holding the bag when market prices fall. Not true. The market maker's purpose is twofold: (1) to facilitate the orderly and available exchange of securities, and (2) to facilitate the orderly and available exchange of securities in a manner profitable to the individual or firm acting as market maker. Part (2) is accomplished through *hedging*, which is defined as taking an opposite or counter balancing position that transfers the risk of loss to an *other party*. The other party is average Americans who invest in a buy and hold strategy that does not provide a hedge or timed entry/exit for their investment monies.

The Problem With Mutual Funds
The mutual fund was created in 1924. Its purpose is to accumulate monies from multiple individuals and invest them in the market or an investable sector in accordance with the fund mission as stipulated in the fund prospectus. A mutual fund cannot deviate from its mission. That is its greatest weakness.

Imagine an army that never retreated to regroup and fight another day. Imagine a basketball coach who never used timeouts when his team was falling behind in order to implement a new game plan. When the advantage in a game is lost, the opportunities and resources to win become fewer. The simple act of pausing the action may be all that is needed to regroup and mount a game-winning change in strategy. This is not possible with mutual funds.

The typical mutual fund loses to fees what advantage it has from the stock picking talents of a good fund manager. Fees are the second weakness of mutual funds. When a fund performs well, it charges a fee. When the fund performs poorly, it still charges that fee.

Recently many have raised their fees because the net investment capital of its participants is inadequate to cover fund expenses, such as management compensation, advertising and promotion, and sales commissions for advisors and planners. For example, a mutual fund that charges 1% on $100,000,000 of participant net capital receives fees totaling $1,000,000. However, when the broad market fell by over 50% on March 9, 2009, the total fees charged at 1% only provided $500,000 of income to cover fund expenses. The mutual fund must raise its fee to 2% to meet the $1,000,000 requirement to cover expenses. *Why is a mutual fund entitled to a fee from its participants after it has lost 30% to 50% of the participants' entrusted monies?*

In few other professional industries in the United States does the customer pay before service is rendered. Imagine a fine restaurant charging before the escargot or fillet mignon is served. The name for such an establishment is a cafeteria. Requesting prepayment for services is an insult, denoting that the client/customer is not valued. The mutual fund company has custody of the participant's monies, rendering incapable the fund participant from skipping out on the bill. *Don't the mutual fund companies trust their customers to pay the fees as billed? Are they worried that because there is a greater probability of the fund underperforming the benchmark rather than meeting or exceeding it, their participants will demand an adjustment in billing due to the fund's poor performance?*

It is hard to lobby for a billing adjustment after one has already paid the bill months or years in advance. The wealthy do not prepay in total all hedge fund management fees. Hedge fund fees are based on performance, and are called performance fees. When the hedge fund performs poorly, the client is not charged a performance fee. *Why don't average American investors receive equal consideration from the mutual fund industry for their investment monies?*

In the financial planning and advisory industry a technique called *rebalancing* is in fashion to counter the third problem with mutual funds, that successful mutual fund managers graduate from mutual funds to the more lucrative hedge fund industry.

If a mutual fund performs well in one year because of its manager's outstanding stock picking abilities, it rarely (though some can) performs well in subsequent years. Rebalancing transfers money from successful mutual funds (the prior year's winners) into unsuccessful mutual funds (the prior year's losers) to attain an equal average dollar value for each fund in a client's portfolio, in the hope that the poor performing funds will introduce new management that can turn them into winners.

This comes with the expectation that highly performing mutual fund managers will move on to the hedge fund industry. The mutual fund friendly explanation of rebalancing claims that because market conditions differ from year to year, poorly performing mutual funds adapt their losing strategies to winning strategies. Issues arising from their explanation follow:

- *What happens when a losing mutual fund adapts its strategy to perform to the parameters of the prior year's market conditions and the market conditions themselves have changed from the prior year to current year? Do some mutual funds never become winners?*
- *Why would a high performing mutual fund be abandoned on the chance that a low performing fund will turn itself into a winner?*
- *How can a strategy that is a 'winner' fail to remain a winner year after year? Does the high performing fund manager understand the market better than the low performing fund manager, or is the high performing fund manager just lucky? If mutual fund success is a function of luck, why would anyone gamble retirement monies by putting them in a mutual fund?*

The fourth problem with mutual funds is that participants' shares can be redeemed only after the market closes--never during market hours. This disadvantages mutual fund participants. When the market opens on bad news in the morning, the fund participants must wait until other investors unload their investments at higher prices before they themselves can exit the market after the close of business, redeeming their mutual fund shares at much lower values. *Is there any disadvantage for the average American greater than this?*

The wealthy do not wait until others exit the market before taking their share. Remember the movie *Titanic*? How it portrayed that there were only enough lifeboats for the 1st class passengers and none for the 2nd and 3rd class passengers. Remember how the 3rd class passengers were shown locked below deck so they could not enjoy the opportunity of survival? It's the same unfair treatment that the average American investor experiences when investing in mutual funds.

The hedge funds employed by the wealthy not only remove them from downside exposure at the first hint of bad news, but also short and leverage the short position to make money as the market falls in multiples of market price declines, not just dollar for dollar.

It is the author's opinion that there has been a lot of misinformation disseminated by the mutual fund industry and its advisory and planning representatives.

The ETF As An Alternative To The Mutual Fund

The better alternative to the mutual fund is the exchange traded fund (ETF). The ETF charges a fraction of the fee that typical mutual funds charge. The ETF is also tradable during market hours, while mutual fund shares are only redeemable for their participants after market close. ETFs can be hedged. ETFs can be leveraged. ETFs can be shorted. ETFs cover all security classes from commodities to bonds. ETFs that are 99% correlated to the benchmark average are available to the public.

The Problem With Bonds

Bond prices are more stable than stock market prices. There are times when bond prices move wildly, a function of Federal Reserve monetary policy and asset price bubble bursts.

If bond prices fall, the investor loses a portion of principal during an early redemption. If bond prices rise (as a function of market forces), the investor gains principal, paying capital gains taxes (possibly at regular income rates) on that principal appreciation even though there is no early redemption (this is only the case for corporate and applicable accreting tax-exempt bonds, but it demonstrates how unfair bond investments can be for the average American).

Alternatively, corporations, municipalities and states can default on their bonds, though less likely for the latter. In 1994 the county of Orange, California, defaulted on its bond issue to a tune of $2,000,000,000.00. Corporations default on bonds more frequently during periods of economic contraction than in periods of economic expansion.

Federal Government issued bonds are backed by the taxing and money printing powers of the United States Treasury. Their bond and bill principal values fluctuate with changes in interest rates. As interest rates rise, the principal value of all fixed income instruments will fall.

Corporate bonds that pay high interest rates are termed *junk bonds*. It may be difficult and expensive to redeem these bonds in the open market without taking a significant sales loss on the price of those bonds (their principal value).

The Bond ETF As An Alternative To The Direct Purchase Bond

The better alternative to a bond is an exchange traded fund (ETF) holding bonds as its portfolio components. The bond ETF provides diversification, ease of purchase and redemption, and low transaction fees.

The Problem With Financial Planners and Financial Advisors

Financial Planners and Financial Advisors frequently recommend to clients not to redeem their shares in mutual funds on a day when the market has fallen, but rather to wait until an 'up' day. *What happens when there are no 'up' days in the market for an entire week?*

That was the case on October 6th to 10th, 2008, when the market's one-week decline was 18.2%, the most since 1933 (not including the 3 'down' days Wednesday through Friday of the prior week, in all totaling a drop of 22.9%). *What happens when clients are advised to wait until the market returns to par (the starting point of losses) before they redeem their mutual fund shares?* That was the likely advice from Financial Planners and Financial Advisors on October 6th 2008. The market continued to fall over the next 6 months to its 12 year and 6 month low on March 9, 2009. This was equal to the September 9th, 1996 high of 676.53, which was 57% percent lower than the recent market highs (October 10th, 2007) and 35.9% lower from the point at which the client originally may have wanted to exit on October 6th, 2008 (as measured by the broad market indicator, the Standard and Poor's 500 Index).

There are two reasons why planners and advisors recommended that clients keep monies invested in mutual funds and market investing variable life insurance policies, rather than remove them to be held as cash. The first is that the planner or advisor is ignorant of market timing technical analysis and indicators that evidenced the market was entering into a recessionary contraction. Conceding the often held opinion that technical analysis is a squirrely science causing even the smartest economists moments of befuddlement, why not accept the fact that the 2008-2009 recession was pre-announced by the Wall Street Journal's "Ahead of the Tape" column on April 4, 2008.

From that point the market had fallen only 14% from the 2007 highs. *Isn't it the job of the planner and advisor to be current with financial news and events? What more could be done to motivate planners and advisors to protect their clients' monies, than for the world's premier financial news outlet to announce that a recession was coming?*

The second reason planners and advisors recommended that clients keep monies invested in mutual funds and market investing variable life insurance policies was for a selfish reason -- they can not bill planning or advisement fees on client monies not invested in the market. *Why is the average American dealing with these self-serving and lazy people? Is there a better alternative?*

The Unfairness Of Life Insurance Annuities

When a life insurance company promises a rate of return on a life insurance annuity, it might not come from fixed income securities such as bonds. It could be from a derivative instrument such as the *swap*. A swap is a contract that facilitates the exchange of one security or its components for another security or its components. It also refers to the exchange of risk or hedging, where the risk of not providing the promised rate of return shifts and becomes another's problem.

Shifting the risk from a life insurance company's contractual obligations is in itself a respectable act. The way it is achieved takes advantage of annuitants, depriving them of other opportunities to obtain higher returns. The insurance company does not disclose how contractual obligation risk is hedged, or how the annuity annual income is derived. If annuitants knew, they would feel deceived. The process is so simple that an annuitant might feel confident enough to attempt the operation on their own.

Here is one of many methods an insurance company uses for fulfilling annuity obligations. It starts with an insurance company customer who wishes to buy a life insurance annuity that will pay an annual income from a deposit of $1,000,000. The insurance company offers an annuity beginning in one year that pays 3% per year. The customer agrees, enters into a contract with the insurance company to become its annuitant and writes a check for $1,000,000.

To accomplish the transfer of risk and to secure a 3% return for the annuitant, the insurance company goes to the hedge fund market and offers to swap the annuitant's $1,000,000 in exchange for a 6% guaranteed return. *Why is a 6% return requested in exchange for the $1,000,000 instead of the 3% return that is promised to the annuitant?* The insurance company, using bankers' mentality, plans to make at least as much money on the annuitant's deposit as the annuitant makes.

All the insurance company has to do to accomplish this transfer of risk through a swap is to find a hedge fund that can make more than 6% a year on principal monies. Even in poor performing markets, this is not a difficult task for a legitimate hedge fund. Here are two examples of how this is accomplished.

(1) Cross-Market Arbitrage: Cross-market arbitrage opportunities that involve miniscule risk exist that return ½% to ¾% per month. Annually, that comes to 6.2% to 9.4%. The hedge fund will instruct the insurance company to deposit a portion of the $1,000,000 into a margin account at a future[s] market exchange and into a margin account at an options market exchange.

The hedge fund will have discretionary trading access within these two margin accounts and will now use future contracts combined with index options at the two exchanges to lock in an arbitrage return, transferring their risk to others in the future and options markets.

Not only is the insurance company taking a return of 3% equal to that of the annuitant, the hedge fund also is taking a 3% return with very little work or risk to itself. A further explanation of this arbitrage strategy will be presented in the forthcoming Hedge Strategies report Cross-Market Arbitrage And Risk-free Trading In The Future, Option And Bond Markets, An Arbitrage Strategy.

(2) Annuity Swap Arbitrage: A second method that a hedge fund uses to hedge the swap obligation is to purchase on margin $1,000,000 of an index through its equivalent such as the individual index stocks that compose the index, or shares of a dividend paying index ETF that mimic the Standard & Poor's 500 Index. The margin stock account will provide 2 to 1 leverage so the hedge fund will control $1,000,000 of index ETF shares with just $500,000. $250,000 will be applied to the margin account at the future exchange, leaving a remaining $250,000 on margin at the stock exchange that will earn interest from fixed income securities (with interest rate risk hedged) to cover margin and trading fees, or will control another $500,000 of index ETFs if desired.

The hedge fund will use its "propriety trading strategies" (similar to the charts and analysis techniques described in the Hedge Strategies report Technical Analysis Techniques For Timing The Market And Trend Trading) to time the market. Explanation of long/short margin ratio hedging is available from Hedge Strategies in its report The Long/Short Margin Ratio Hedge.

It will use 4 index future contracts on the Standard & Poor's 500 Index, requiring at most a margin deposit of $25,000 for each future contract (each future contract controls roughly $250,000; 4 contracts control roughly $1,000,000). The hedge fund can then hedge the $1,000,000 index ETF share position by shorting 4 index future contracts that will zero out any index ETF share losses. The short future contract hedge will be removed when the market is trending up, allowing the ETF shares to profit.

The hedge fund may double its up trend gains by adding to the long index ETF shares with 4 long future contracts. Now $2,000,000 of the index is controlled with just $600,000.

At time of this writing, the Standard & Poor's 500 Index pays a dividend of 2.25%, nearly covering the annuity amount promised to the annuitant, leaving just 3.75% that must be covered before the hedge fund makes income for itself.

The insurance company makes a profit of $30,000. The annuitant receives $30,000 that year from the $1,000,000 annuity. The hedge fund can improve its returns by inverting its strategy to a -2 to +1 ratio with a net short position of -1 when the market trend is bearish.

The terms of the swap contract may require that the risk of loss be hedged to zero at all times whenever annuity deposit monies are exposed to market risk. This means that the hedge fund will keep the 4 shorted index future contracts active while the index ETF shares are in the market.

When the market falls, profit is harvested from the 4 shorted index future contracts. The process is called *rolling a contract* and involves closing the 4 shorted index future contracts position for a profit, while simultaneously shorting another 4 index future contracts that are lower priced, compared to the current appreciated price of the first 4. When the trend changes from bearish to bullish, a portion of the short future profit can be applied to the purchase of a long put in the options market (this is the only instance that the purchase of a put hedge will be advised by Hedge Strategies), and the short future position can be removed leaving just the long leveraged ETF investment.

Rolling the contract harvests profit from the money-making short future positions, which can now be applied to a multitude of money-making possibilities that will profit when the market moves up, such as long index future contracts, options on long index future contracts, options on index ETF shares or leveraged ETF shares. The annuitant receives the promised 3%, the life insurance company receives their 3% and the hedge fund makes many times the obligated percentages—accomplished entirely with the annuitant's $1,000,000 deposit.

The profit potential for hedge funds on swap contracts is enormous, whether on fully hedged strategies or those strategies that tolerate more risk. Perhaps one should not be so thankful to life insurance companies for the rate of return on their annuities, especially if they do not explain how the annuity amount will be invested.

Automatic Trading
The Best Alternative For Clients Of Investment Advisors & Financial Planners
Automatic trading is the safe alternative to financial planners and investment advisors who place client monies into high commission poor performing mutual funds, or place their own interests ahead of their client interests by leaving client investment monies exposed to risk during down-trending market cycles so they can continue to bill and collect fees from them.

Automatic trading frequently sends advanced derivative trading instructions to the brokerage firm in possession of client investment accounts, so clients are able to realize profits when prudent or hedge against losses when the market falls. These are the benefits for subscribers to skilled automatic trading services:

1) Client monies always remain in the client investment account. Only the brokerage firm and client have control over those monies. The automatic trading service never takes possession of client monies, and never assumes control over the client account in any way beyond the trading instructions that are transmitted to the brokerage firm for submission to the market per the client's authorization. The client brokerage firm is responsible for proper trading order entry.

2) Clients have access to a professional brokerage trading platform. The advantages of this trading platform includes:

    i) Very low trading fees and commissions. Derivative trading fees are as low as $0.70 per contract and commissions on stocks are as low as $0.005 per share.

    ii) Average price executions are available in addition to flat price executions. This is a method professionals use to move their order in front of flat price orders, increasing the probability that their order will be filled first.

    iii) Algorithm positioning only fills an order if it is at the absolute best available price that moment. If a better price is available the algorithm converts the order price to the better price and fills it.

    iv) Pre-market and after-hours trading allows the client to get into or get out of an investment or position when news breaks outside of regular trading hours.

3) Fees are never billed in advance of performance. Fees are only billed after a performance-measuring period. If negative performance occurs, no fee is billed.

4) The client has multiple strategies to choose from that can be applied to his/her investment account. Each strategy has unique reward to risk characteristics.

5) The reward to risk of each strategy is clearly defined and statistically reliable.

6) Automatic trading can be cancelled any time at the client's discretion.

Linked Trading
Similar to automatic trading, linked trading simultaneously submits to the market the same trading instruction for the client account that is entered and submitted in a hedge fund's master account.

Linked trading removes the possibility of delayed order entry and incorrect order entry by the brokerage firm in possession of the client account.

An added benefit from this type of automatic trading is that the buying power of multiple accounts is combined to create a larger market footprint -- increasing derivative profit opportunities.

www.ingramcontent.com/pod-product-compliance
Lightning Source LLC
Chambersburg PA
CBHW050425180526
45159CB00005B/2413